·CORONATION ST.· ™

THE OFFICIAL
COLOURING BOOK
colour classic scenes from the show's history

hamlyn

An Hachette UK Company
www.hachette.co.uk

First published in Great Britain in 2016 by Hamlyn, a division of
Octopus Publishing Group Ltd
Carmelite House, 50 Victoria Embankment
London EC4Y 0DZ
www.octopusbooks.co.uk

Coronation Street is an ITV Studios Production

Distributed in Canada by
Canadian Manda Group
664 Annette St.
Toronto, Ontario, Canada M6S 2C8

ISBN 978 0 600 63463 8

A CIP catalogue record for this book is available from the British Library

Printed and bound in China

3 5 7 9 10 8 6 4 2

Editorial Director: Trevor Davies
Designer: Jaz Bahra
Editor: Natalie Bradley
Contributor: Glenda Young
Proofreader: Emma Hill
Production Controller: Sarah Kulasek-Boyd

Artworks created by:
260 Danny @ KJA-Artists.com
132 Nick @ KJA-Artists.com

CONTENTS

INTRODUCTION

Coronation Street first aired live at 7pm on Friday 9 December 1960. It was created by a young scriptwriter called Tony Warren. Tony sat on top of a filing cabinet in the office of Granada TV executive Harry Elton, and refused to come down until Harry allowed him to write about what he knew best – the North of England. Tony was told to get down and return the next day with a programme. He had already written two scripts based on life in an ordinary street and he combined both scripts within 24 hours and presented his idea to Harry Elton about a new show called *Florizel Street*. The title was changed to *Coronation Street* after a Granada tea lady called Agnes said that Florizel sounded like a disinfectant.

Back then, the television establishment feared that viewers would not watch this new cutting-edge drama serial about the ordinary, day-to-day lives of working-class northerners. A Granada TV executive feared if the show was transmitted that advertisers would withdraw their advertising. And when the pilot episodes were shown, one television critic even went as far as to write: 'The programme is doomed from the outset… with its dreary signature tune and grim scenes of a row of terraced houses and smoking chimneys. For there is little reality in this new serial, which apparently, we have to suffer twice a week.'

How wrong the doubters were! Now, more than half a century and over 9,000 episodes later, the television show about the everyday lives of ordinary folk in a northern town called Weatherfield has gone on to become the most successful and best-loved drama serial in the world. Not only that, *Coronation Street* changed the face of British television and set the standard which other serial dramas now follow.

Over the years, viewers and fans of the show have laughed, cried and shared the highs and lows of the characters who have been brought to life in their living rooms. *Coronation Street*'s unique blend of heart-warming comedy, powerful drama, fascinating characters and superb scriptwriting is now shown in more than 40 countries around the world. The award-winning show takes its rightful place in television history as the world's longest-running drama serial.

Through all of its years, *Coronation Street* has moved with the times whilst retaining its unique sense of northern humour. It is a show filled with pathos, tragedy, conflict and drama. However, at the heart of the drama, are ordinary people trying to overcome adversity. The strong women, feckless men and families remain the focus of the show, following the groundbreaking template set by Tony Warren decades ago. It is as realistic and truthful as a television drama can be, it entertains and amuses and shows us characters we can identify with and care about. The show remains on our screens because it feels like a friend. Very often viewers will have formed an affection for it in their childhood or when they were going through a dramatic period in their life. So when they return to it, it's like returning to an old friend. It's there, it's safe and it's secure.

The pictures in this wonderful book feature lots of *Coronation Street*'s classic characters and storyline highlights since the very beginning through to the present day. Relive classic moments, unforgettable villains, favourite quotes and the best soap queens. We hope that you enjoy this trip down memory lane and that some of your favourite scenes are included in our pick of the most explosive, amusing and heartfelt storylines from the history of the show.

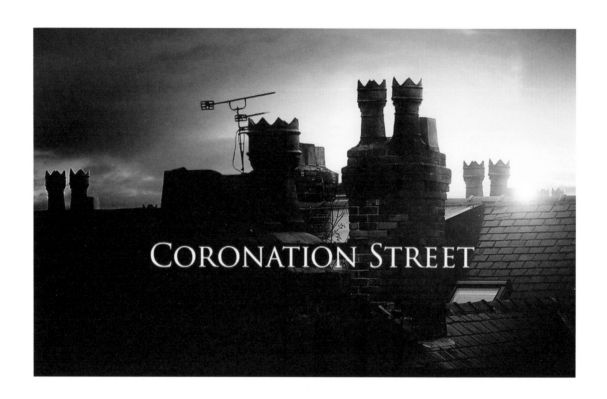

CORONATION STREET OPENING

· ·

From the very first episode on Friday 9 December 1960, *Coronation Street*'s opening titles have included the rooftops, chimney pots, cobbles and terraced streets of Weatherfield.

Rovers Return landlady Annie Walker once declared the view to be of: '… blackened chimneys piercing the sultry sky like jagged teeth'. Sheer poetry!

The original title sequence was filmed in Archie Street, Salford, which was demolished in 1971. The opening titles we currently see on screen were introduced in May 2010. Cue the familiar theme tune – turn the page and settle in for a nostalgic trip down memory lane…

FIRST EPISODE (1960)

· ·

Elsie Tanner, played by Pat Phoenix, was one of the original *Coronation Street* characters. She was the first siren of the Street, the show's original tart with a heart. Elsie was a headstrong, passionate and wilful woman with an eye for the fellas, too. In 23 years on the Street, Elsie entertained 20 men and married 3 of them. Her golden rule was never to mess with another woman's man, but the women on the Street still marked Elsie as a threat. Elsie's flame-haired beauty was just a little too exotic for Weatherfield ways.

In this scene, Elsie sits at a table in her living room and surveys her reflection in the mirror.
'Eeh, Elsie. You're just about ready for the knacker yard.'

MINNIE, ENA AND MARTHA (1961)

Minnie Caldwell, Ena Sharples and Martha Longhurst formed a formidable trio of *Coronation Street*'s older ladies. They liked to meet for a gossip and a glass of milk stout in the snug at the Rovers Return.

Ena was the show's original battleaxe, a harridan in a hairnet who often bullied her friend, the timid, cat-loving Minnie. Despite their waspish bickering, the three women remained friends until Martha passed away after suffering a heart attack in the snug in 1964.

Musing on death, Ena once said: 'I would just like to go the way me mother did. She just sat up, broke wind, and died.'

Left to right: Minnie Caldwell [Margot Bryant], Ena Sharples [Violet Carson] and Martha Longhurst [Lynne Carol].

CHRISTMAS AT THE
ROVERS RETURN (1967)

Weatherfield knows how to enjoy a festive knees-up. Proving that the Rovers Return has always known how to throw a great party, here is a group of the regulars enjoying a sing-along at Christmas 1967.

With Ena Sharples playing the pub piano, many of the *Coronation Street* regulars are pictured in party mode. On the piano sits Elsie Tanner surrounded by Stan and Hilda Ogden, Emily Nugent and the Rovers' landlord and landlady Jack and Annie Walker.

Left to right: Lucille Hewitt [Jennifer Moss], Minnie Caldwell [Margot Bryant], Stan Ogden [Bernard Youens], Annie Walker [Doris Speed], Ena Sharples [Violet Carson], Emily Nugent [Eileen Derbyshire], Jerry Booth [Graham Haberfield], Jack Walker [Arthur Leslie], Hilda Ogden [Jean Alexander], Steve Tanner [Paul Maxwell] and Elsie Tanner [Patricia Phoenix].

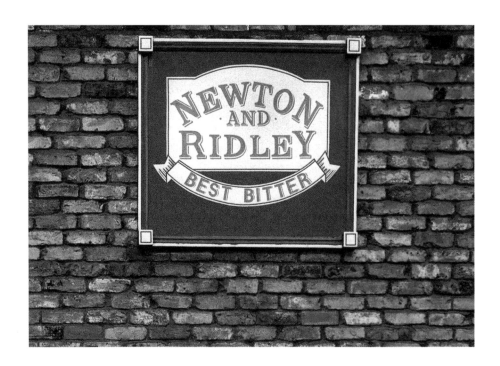

NEWTON AND RIDLEY

. . . .

Newton and Ridley is the brewery which has been supplying beer to the Rovers Return since the programme began. The brewery was owned and operated by Cecil Newton and Nigel Ridley. It also supplies beer to the Rovers' rival pubs The Flying Horse and The Weatherfield Arms.

Newton and Ridley twice attempted to rebrand the Rovers. They wanted to turn it into a fun pub called The Boozy Newt and again as a yuppie bar called Yankees. However, the brewery faced stiff opposition from the Weatherfield locals and the pub has always remained as the Rovers Return Inn.

BETTY AND ANNIE IN
THE ROVERS RETURN (1975)

Rovers landlady Annie Walker was a first-class snob. She saw the Rovers as her empire, her royal domain. When the pub threw a Silver Jubilee party in 1977, Annie dressed up as Queen Elizabeth I, telling Albert Tatlock: 'You can't rehearse majesty, Mr Tatlock. Either you've got it or you haven't.' Annie is pictured here with Betty Turpin, one of the Rovers' best-loved barmaids – and the longest serving. Betty introduced her famous hotpot to the pub's lunchtime menu. The legendary hotpot remains a favourite with the regulars to this very day.

Left to right: Betty Turpin [Betty Driver], Annie Walker [Doris Speed].

HILDA OGDEN AND THE 'MURIEL' (1976)

Eddie Yeats wallpapered Stan and Hilda Ogden's back room with a mural of the Canadian Rockies in 1976. He told Hilda: 'That's your scenic panorama contrast wall that is. Dead trendy that. Latest there is!'

Little did Eddie know that Hilda's mural, or 'muriel', as she always called it, would become such a design classic. Hilda gave the mural her classic touch when she hung three flying ducks on it.

The iconic flying ducks first appeared in *Coronation Street* on the living room wall at No. 11, Elsie Tanner's house.

Left to right: Hilda Ogden [Jean Alexander], Eddie Yeats [Geoffrey Hughes], Stan Ogden [Bernard Youens].

THE CORONATION STREET
OLYMPICS (1984)

· ·

The Rovers Return went into competition with rival pub The Flying Horse when they staged their own version of The Olympics in 1984. Annie Walker's son Billy organized the event to raise funds for Emily Bishop's church appeal. Percy Sugden wanted to be in charge of the Olympics Committee but had his nose pushed out when Alf Roberts was appointed to head it instead. At the Olympics, Betty Turpin proved to be a champion at wellie-wanging. 'How d'you get muscles like that?' she was asked. 'Practice!' she replied. 'Chuckin' folk out the Rovers!'

Here's Bet Lynch, Hilda Ogden and Vera Duckworth looking determined to beat The Flying Horse in the egg and spoon race.

Left to right: Bet Lynch [Julie Goodyear], Hilda Ogden [Jean Alexander] and Vera Duckworth [Liz Dawn].

THE ROVERS RETURN INN

· ·

The Rovers Return is the most iconic public house on British TV. It is the hub of the community of Coronation Street, where drama unfolds in the bar, and tears are shed in the back room.

Since *Coronation Street* began, this famous backstreet boozer has witnessed wakes and weddings, births and deaths, crashes, fires and fights. And like every historic pub, it has been rumoured to have its own ghost.

Over the years, legendary landladies such as Liz McDonald, Bet Gilroy and Annie Walker have all served up drinks and hotpots along with wisdom and advice from behind the bar.

BETTABUYS – TROUBLE IN STORE (1989)

....

Norman 'Curly' Watts started work as trainee assistant manager at Bettabuys supermarket in 1989. As Curly was lodging with Vera and Jack Duckworth at the time, Vera used her position as Curly's landlady to get herself a job shelf-stacking at Bettabuys. However, Vera's antics soon resulted in her being sacked by supermarket boss Reg Holdsworth. After Curly found Reg in a compromising position with the store detective in the stock room, he blackmailed Reg into giving Vera her job back. And it was while working at Bettabuys that Curly found romance with shelf-stacker Kimberley Taylor.

Left to right: Vera Duckworth [Liz Dawn], Reg Holdsworth [Ken Morley], Kimberley Taylor [Suzanne Hall] and Curly Watts [Kevin Kennedy].

THE LOVE BIRDS – MAVIS AND DEREK (1994)

· ·

Mavis and Derek Wilton were one of *Coronation Street*'s best-loved couples. Always dithering, the two of them finally decided to marry after an eight-year courtship. But on the day of their wedding in 1984, they both got cold feet and neither turned up at the church. It would take another four years before they were eventually wed. During their courtship Derek beat his love rival Victor Pendlebury in the battle to win Mavis' heart.

'You've a lot in common with Marilyn Monroe,' Derek told her once. 'You're not aware of the power of your own sexuality, Mavis.'

Left to right: Derek Wilton [Peter Baldwin] and Mavis Wilton [Thelma Barlow].

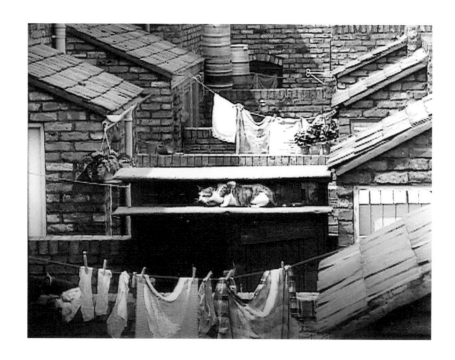

THE CORONATION STREET CAT

The *Coronation Street* cat appeared regularly in the programme titles. The Street cat became so popular with viewers of the show that when the time came to update the opening sequence, a competition was held on ITV's *This Morning* programme to cast a new cat to star in the new clips. *Coronation Street* received more than 5,000 applications from cat owners. The winning cat, Frisky (pictured here), starred in the *Coronation Street* opening titles from 1990 to 2002.

STAR-CROSSED LOVERS (1994)

· ·

In an attempt to impress his bosses at supermarket SoopaScoopa, Curly Watts pretended
to be engaged and asked Raquel Wolstenhulme to pose as his fiancée, which she duly did.
He was in love with Raquel long before the pretend engagement, and this infatuation
eventually drove him to propose to her for real. Raquel accepted, even though she knew
she didn't truly love him. To mark their engagement in 1994, Curly named a star after
his future wife – Mrs Raquel Watts. Curly and Raquel were married a year later in
Coronation Street's 35th anniversary show. However, Raquel soon left Curly to live abroad.
They were reunited in January 2000 in a *Coronation Street* Millennium special episode,
featuring only Curly and Raquel.

Left to right: Curly Watts [Kevin Kennedy] and Raquel Wolstenhulme [Sarah Lancashire].

BET GILROY LEAVES
THE ROVERS RETURN (1995)

Bet Gilroy, played by Julie Goodyear, is one of the most iconic barmaids and pub landladies that the Rovers Return has ever had. With her trademark leopard print, beehive and earrings, she proved a force to be reckoned with when she was behind the bar and running the pub.

However, when Newton and Ridley announced that they were selling off some of their public houses, including the Rovers Return, Bet didn't have the money to buy her beloved pub. She asked Rita for a loan, but Rita refused to help and the two of them had a major falling-out.

This led to Bet leaving *Coronation Street* in 1995, although she returned briefly in 2002.

JACK AND VERA TAKE OVER THE ROVERS (1995)

Having worked as the pub's potman, it was a dream come true for Jack Duckworth to be able to buy the Rovers Return. Using an inheritance from his brother Cliff, the Duckworths became the new landlords of their local boozer. However, it was Vera's name that went up above the door as landlady, due to Jack's previous run-ins with the police. When the Duckies took over the pub, barmaid Betty walked out in a row over her hotpot and they had to grovel to get her back. Jack and Vera called time behind the bar when they fell foul of the tax man over an unpaid bill and Jack sold the pub to Alec Gilroy.

Left to right: Vera Duckworth [Liz Dawn] and Jack Duckworth [Bill Tarmey].

BETTY AND MARMADUKE
THE CAT (1995)

....

Betty Turpin, played by Betty Driver, had a year of mixed fortunes in 1995. She bumped into
an old flame called Billy Williams who invited her to a tea dance. Billy confessed that he had
thought about her fondly and often over the years. Then, when Betty's home was burgled it was
Billy who helped Betty cope. He proposed marriage, twice, and finally Betty accepted him and
the two of them were married. After Billy died of a heart attack, Betty spent more time working
at the Rovers while her cat Marmaduke provided comfort at home.

FRED ELLIOTT, I SAY, FRED! (1995)

Fred Elliott was the larger-than-life butcher of the street. He had a habit of repeating everything he said and liked to drink 'Scotch and Threat' in the pub.

Fred, played by John Savident, was hiding a family secret when he first appeared in *Coronation Street*. He eventually revealed that his nephew, Ashley Peacock, was really his biological son. Fortunately, once he got over the shock, Ashley – I say, Ashley – reacted well to the news that Fred was his dad and a new sign went up at the butcher shop – Elliott & Son.

A serial proposer, Fred was finally accepted by Bev Unwin. However, on his wedding day to Bev, en route to the church, Fred died in Audrey Roberts' hallway. His last words? 'Be happy, I say, be happy.'

KEVIN WEBSTER'S AFFAIR (1997)

When brazen Natalie Horrocks arrived in Coronation Street she seduced garage mechanic Kevin Webster while his wife Sally was looking after her mother in Scarborough. Kevin fell for Natalie and planned to leave Sally and his young daughters Rosie and Sophie. When Sally returned to Weatherfield and discovered what had been going on, she stormed out of No. 13 to find Natalie. And when she did find her, Sally gave Natalie one of the best slaps that *Coronation Street* has ever seen.

Rita Sullivan later made her feelings about Natalie quite clear during a heated exchange, in which she told her: 'By hell, lady – I've met some hard-faced bitches in my time, but you take the bloody gold medal!'

Left to right: Sally Webster [Sally Dynevor] and Natalie Horrocks [Denise Welch].

THE BATTERSBYS ARRIVE (1997)

The residents of Coronation Street didn't know what had hit them when the rough-and-ready Battersby family moved into No. 5 in 1997. Brash and common, the Battersbys drove their neighbours mad by playing loud music. When Curly Watts broke in and threw their CD player onto the cobbles, Les Battersby head-butted him and broke Curly's glasses. Percy Sugden started a petition to have the Battersbys removed and Rovers Return landlord Alec Gilroy was among those less than impressed with the new arrivals. 'Les Battersby's a beast in human form,' Alec huffed. 'Well, almost human form…'

Left to right: Toyah [Georgia Taylor], Les [Bruce Jones], Janice [Vicky Entwistle] and Leanne Battersby [Jane Danson].

FREE THE WEATHERFIELD ONE (1998)

When Deirdre Rachid fell for fake pilot Jon Lindsay she ended up in court on a fraud trial. In a miscarriage of justice, Deirdre was wrongly found guilty and sent down for 18 months. When she was given the sentence, she cried out to the judge: 'I didn't do any of it!'

Over 18 million viewers watched as Deirdre, played by Anne Kirkbride, was wrongly sent to prison. The storyline resulted in a huge public response and the campaign to Free the Weatherfield One was launched. Questions were even asked in Parliament!

With Mike Baldwin leading the campaign to free Deirdre, and the support of her friends in Weatherfield, Deirdre's innocence was proved and she was freed after just three weeks inside.

THE KABIN – RITA AND NORRIS (1999)

In 1999 Rita Sullivan took on a new assistant in The Kabin when Norris Cole approached her for a job after his divorce from wife Angela. Rita was only too happy to take on Norris. She needed a replacement for Blanche Hunt who, it was fair to say, was less than cheerful working in customer service. Rita's new sidekick Norris was a welcome addition to the newsagent shop.

Over the years, Norris and Rita have rubbed along nicely working together. There's a strong friendship between them, although Norris often gets on Rita's nerves.

Norris once popped the question to Rita, but she turned down his proposal flat.

Left to right: Norris Cole [Malcolm Hebden], Blanche Hunt [Maggie Jones] and Rita Sullivan [Barbara Knox].

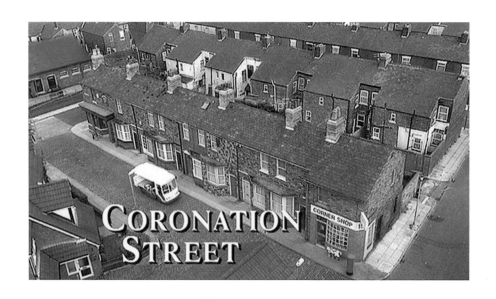

CORONATION STREET
OPENING TITLES

· ·

Coronation Street's opening titles from 2002 give a good overview of the Street itself and beyond. In these rows of terraced houses and cobbled streets on which the milkman makes his morning rounds, we are given a secret glimpse into Weatherfield life. At one end is Rosamund Street – home to the Medical Centre and the chip shop – and at the other is Viaduct Street. Tucked away behind Coronation Street is the often referred to but rarely seen Mawdsley Street.

GAIL MARRIES
RICHARD HILLMAN (2002)

It's fair to say that *Coronation Street*'s Gail is no stranger to wedding cake. It's also true that she's had a complicated history with men. By the time she married Richard Hillman in 2002 she had already worked her way through two husbands – Brian Tilsley (whom she married not once, but twice!) and Martin Platt. So, would it be third time lucky for Gail when she married Richard Hillman? Well, he certainly seemed nice. He was charming, loving and, above all else, Richard Hillman was a family man. What could possibly go wrong?

Left to right: Richard Hillman [Brian Capron] and Gail Hillman [Helen Worth].

RICHARD TRIES TO KILL
THE PLATTS (2003)

Oh 'eck. It didn't take Gail long to discover that new husband Richard Hillman was a murderer and a con man. Over 19 million viewers tuned in to watch Richard's confession to Gail. 'Everything I've done, I've done for you,' he told her. 'I've killed for you, Gail. Did Martin or Brian love you that much?'

Deranged Richard then bundled Gail, David, Sarah-Lou and Bethany into his car and drove straight into the canal. 'I LOVE YOU!' he screamed as the car leapt off the canal-path and plunged into the water. The Platt family survived but Richard drowned in a watery grave.

SCHMEICHEL WANTS A PIZZA THE ACTION (2004)

· ·

Cilla Brown and Les Battersby decided that a Hawaiian night was just what was needed to christen their new jacuzzi. They splashed out and bought pineapple-topped pizza to eat in the bath. As the couple were enjoying the soapy bubbles, Chesney, Kirk and Fiz returned from a walk with Schmeichel the Great Dane. As soon as Schmeichel came into the house he caught a whiff of the pizza smell coming from the bathroom. The dog bounded upstairs and jumped into the bath to get at the food. But with the extra weight of the dog in the bath, it collapsed through the bathroom floor! A dazed Cilla and Les, along with Schmeichel and some very soapy pizza all ended up in the Battersbys' front room.

Left to right: Les Battersby [Bruce Jones], Schmeichel the Great Dane and Cilla Brown [Wendi Peters].

DEV AND SUNITA'S WEDDING (2004)

· ·

Shopkeeper Dev Alahan married Sunita Parekh in a lavish Hindu wedding ceremony. Dev arrived for the wedding at the Hindu temple resplendent on horseback and in traditional attire. However, as Dev and Sunita were exchanging vows their day was cut short when the police stormed in and arrested Sunita for bigamy! Behind it all was Dev's spurned ex-girlfriend 'mad Maya' who had married several illegal immigrants using Sunita's name. When Maya was rumbled, she went on a rampage, setting all of Dev's shops ablaze and blowing them up.

Left to right: Sunita Parekh [Shobna Gulati], Shelley Unwin [Sally Lindsay] and Dev Alahan [Jimmi Harkishin].

CRUEL CHARLIE STUBBS (2005)

Charlie Stubbs the builder was a nasty piece of work. He was a controlling, manipulative, cheating bully who played cruel mind-games on fiancée Shelley Unwin. He also slept with her mother, Bev. However, Shelley allowed herself to get carried away in their wedding preparations. Until, that is, she was forced to listen to a few home truths about Charlie. On their wedding day, Shelley arrived late at the church, unsure what she was going to do. When the vicar asked her: 'Do you take this man?' she blurted out: 'No! I'm sorry, I don't!' before doing a runner in her wedding dress all the way back to Coronation Street.

Left to right: Shelley Unwin [Sally Lindsay] and Charlie Stubbs [Bill Ward].

THE SHOPS OF
CORONATION STREET (2006)

The Kabin and Dev Alahan's Corner Shop aren't just places to buy sweets, pay the papers, or pop in for a packet of biscuits for the Streetcars office. No – they're much more than that! These are the shops where secrets are revealed and blackmail takes place. There's even a ghost haunting the back room of The Kabin – or so Norris once thought.

Both the Corner Shop and The Kabin were badly damaged in the tram crash of 2010. After repair work, Norris reopened the Kabin as 'Norris's News'. Rita was distraught until the shop name was changed back. And over the road at the corner shop, Molly Dobbs died in the disaster when the tram crashed down from the viaduct onto the Street.

BY 'ECK, IT'S ECCLES! (2006)

When Blanche Hunt's friend Lena Thistlewood died she left her Border Terrier, called Lady Freckles, to Blanche in her will. But Blanche's great-granddaughter Amy Barlow couldn't pronounce the dog's name properly and so they changed it to Eccles. At No. 1 Coronation Street Deirdre and Eccles got on like old pals. Deirdre took the dog with her for company on her ciggie breaks in the ginnel.

Eccles caused waves in the Barlow marriage when the dog fell into the canal. Ken rescued Eccles with the help of barge owner Martha Fraser. Ken and Martha became lovers and he contemplated leaving Deirdre, and Weatherfield behind.

Sharp-tongued Blanche once told her daughter Deirdre: 'Good looks are a curse. You and Ken should count yourselves very lucky.'

Left to right: Blanche Hunt [Maggie Jones] and Deirdre Barlow [Anne Kirkbride] with Eccles the dog.

SHOWTIME AT THE
ROVERS RETURN (2006)

Karaoke nights at the Rovers Return give the pub regulars the chance to show off their singing skills. Whether it's crooning or caterwauling, the residents of Coronation Street love a night of entertainment in their favourite pub.

And the Rovers is no stranger to putting on a show. Over the years the pub has hosted strip shows, talent shows, acts of clairvoyance, plays and pantomimes.

Here are Deirdre Barlow, Rovers landlady Liz McDonald and Eileen Grimshaw up on stage belting out their rendition of The Weather Girls' legendary hit 'It's Raining Men'.

Left to right: Deirdre Barlow [Anne Kirkbride], Liz McDonald [Beverley Callard] and Eileen Grimshaw [Sue Cleaver].

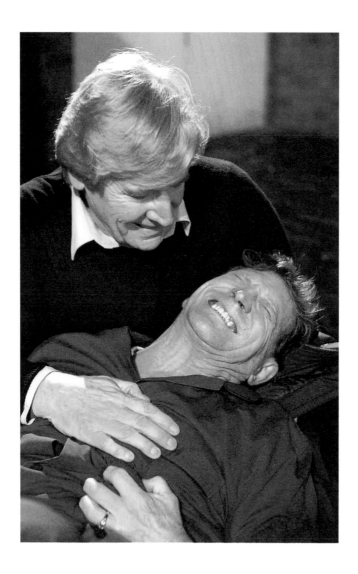

MIKE DIES IN KEN'S ARMS (2006)

Wheeler-dealer Mike Baldwin and retired school teacher Ken Barlow were rivals for decades. Ken never forgave Mike for his affair with Deirdre and there was no love lost between them. Soon after Mike was diagnosed with Alzheimer's Disease, Ken found Mike slumped outside the factory and rang for an ambulance. As they waited for the emergency services to arrive, Ken cradled Mike in his arms. Mike's body slumped backwards as the life drained from him. The man who had for so much of Ken's life been his sworn enemy was now lying dead in his arms.

When sharp-tongued Blanche found out that Mike had passed away she was less than sympathetic. 'I bet Deirdre's glad she picked Ken, now!'

Left to right: Ken Barlow [William Roache] and Mike Baldwin [Johnny Briggs].

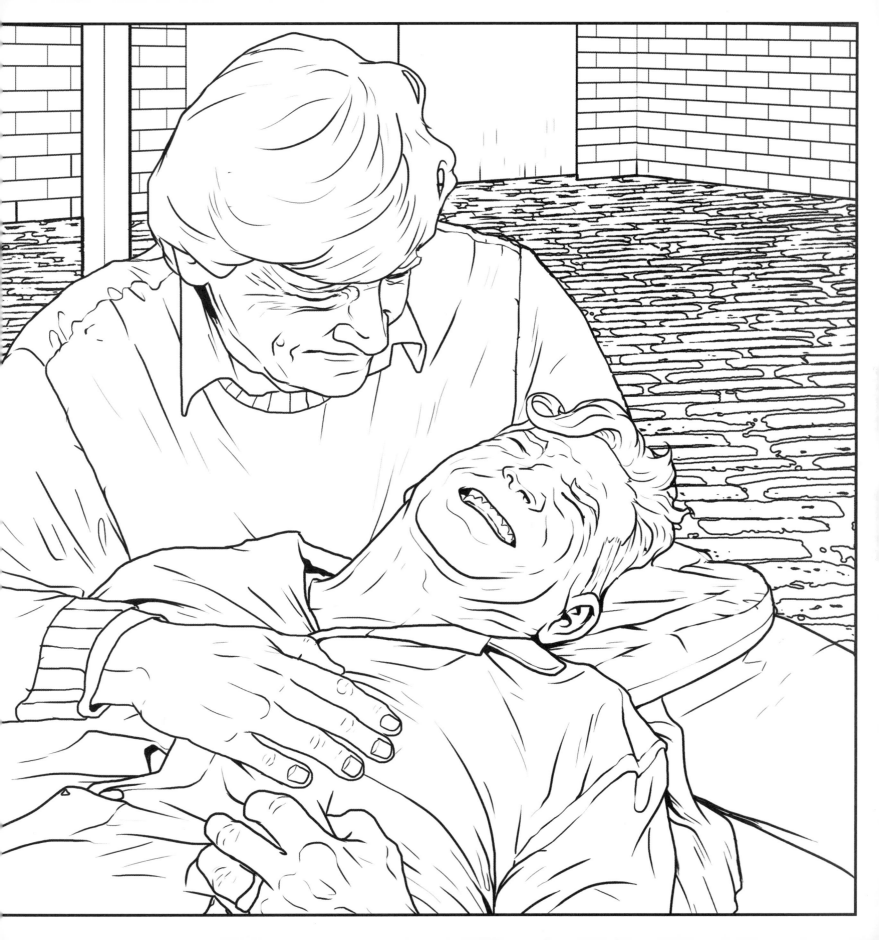

LIFE'S GRIM FOR
THE GRIMSHAWS (2007)

On Christmas Day in 2006, a young woman called Emma knocked at the door of No. 11 Coronation Street. Emma was cradling a baby in her arms and she handed the infant to Eileen, claiming that Jason was the baby's dad. However, Emma had slept with Jason's boss, evil Charlie Stubbs, who had told Emma his name was Jason Grimshaw! Despite this, Eileen bonded with the baby and initially refused to give the child back to Emma. Eileen went as far as trying to convince herself and others that Emma was an unfit mother. After a change of heart, Eileen eventually handed the baby over to Social Services.

Left to right: Jason Grimshaw [Ryan Thomas] and Eileen Grimshaw [Sue Cleaver].

LLOYD FALLS FOR STEVE'S MUM (2009)

Best mates Steve McDonald and Lloyd Mullaney had a major falling-out in 2009 when Steve's mum Liz starting dating Lloyd. Lloyd tried to keep his fling with older woman Liz a secret – but Steve soon found out and was horrified! After a few months, Liz dumped Lloyd when she went to visit son Andy in Spain. When Liz returned from Spain in her flamenco frock, she had some explaining to do.

Liz and Lloyd enjoyed a brief reunion in 2015 before Lloyd left the cobbles for good to start a new life with his pregnant girlfriend Andrea.

Left to right: Lloyd Mullaney [Craig Charles], Liz McDonald [Beverley Callard] and Steve McDonald [Simon Gregson].

TRAM CRASH! (2010)

Coronation Street celebrated its 50th anniversary in December 2010 with an explosive, dramatic live episode. The hard-hitting anniversary episode brought carnage to the cobbles as devastation and disaster hit Weatherfield. The live episode follows the aftermath of a gas explosion at The Old Joinery, which caused a passing tram to derail from the viaduct above the Street. The residents looked on in horror as the tram crashed down to the cobbles and ploughed into the corner shop. Ashley Peacock and Molly Dobbs were killed in the explosion and tram crash while Peter Barlow and Rita Sullivan were rushed to hospital with serious injuries.

GARY'S POST-TRAUMATIC STRESS DISORDER (2011)

Izzy Armstrong was delighted when boyfriend Gary Windass told her he had a surprise for her. But when Gary revealed he'd got himself a job at Underworld, the knicker-stitching factory where Izzy worked, so they could spend more time together, Izzy felt suffocated. Gary soon became over-protective of Izzy and refused to let her leave the house. What Izzy's workmates at the factory didn't know was that Gary was battling the effects of post-traumatic stress disorder. Gary had been injured serving in the army while on deployment in Helmand Province, where his mate Quinny died.

Foreground left to right: Izzy Armstrong [Cherylee Houston] and Julie Carp [Katy Cavanagh]. Background left to right:
Gary Windass [Mikey North], Kirk Sutherland [Andrew Whyment], Sally Webster [Sally Dynevor] and Sean Tully [Antony Cotton].

PLATT FAMILY SECRETS (2011)

Audrey Roberts runs the hairdressing salon, employing her grandson David Platt as a stylist. David's new wife Kylie joined the team to run a nail bar in 2011. Despite having their feet firmly under the table at Gail's house, Kylie wanted to move into the salon flat. She insisted that Audrey evict Maria Connor so that she and David could move in. Audrey refused Kylie's demand. David and Kylie stayed on at Gail's where their expanding family outgrew the available space. They decided to build an annexe for Gail, and a manhole under the floor proved the perfect hiding place for the dead body of drug dealer Callum Logan in 2015.

Left to right: David Platt [Jack P Shepherd], Audrey Roberts [Sue Nicholls] and Kylie Platt [Paula Lane].

HAPPY FAMILIES? (2012)

Poor little Simon Barlow. He was passed from pillar to post while his dad Peter battled his addiction to alcohol – and women. When Peter dated Carla Connor, Simon lied to Leanne that Carla had been hitting him. In the back room of the Rovers, Leanne promised Simon that she'd never let Carla hurt him again. But when Peter arrived to find out what Simon had been saying, he insisted Carla hadn't done anything wrong and urged Simon to tell the truth. Eventually they coaxed the truth out of him. But when Simon admitted he made it all up to get rid of Carla, it broke Peter's heart.

Left to Right: Peter Barlow [Chris Gascoyne], Simon Barlow [Alex Bain] and Leanne Barlow [Jane Danson].

TOGETHER IN BLACKPOOL (2013)

Roy and Hayley Cropper are one of the best-loved couples in the history of *Coronation Street*. After transsexual Hayley was diagnosed with pancreatic cancer, she decided to make the most of the time she had left. She told Roy she wanted to spend a day in Blackpool. Roy and Hayley were full of love for each other as they agreed to forget the 'c' word and enjoy their day by the sea. They visited the arcade, paddled in the sea, ate candy floss and had their fortunes told. After a tram ride and a walk on the pier they headed to the Tower Ballroom for a spot of dancing.

Left to right: Hayley Cropper [Julie Hesmondhalgh] and Roy Cropper [David Neilson].

TROUBLESOME TONY (2014)

Eileen Grimshaw's ex, Tony Stewart, returned to Coronation Street and Liz McDonald fell for him in a big way. The chemistry between Liz and Tony was clear for all to see. They were like a couple of excitable teenagers. And it wasn't long before Liz asked him to move into the Rovers. However, she soon found out that Tony was having an affair with Tracy Barlow. To add insult to injury, Tony and Tracy were planning to steal the Rovers from under her nose. When Liz found out the truth, Tony was unceremoniously dumped. Poor Liz… she's never had much luck with men.

Left to right: Liz McDonald [Beverley Callard] and Tony Stewart [Terence Maynard].

TYRONE AND FIZ (2014)

Life seemed to lurch from one disaster to another for Tyrone Dobbs and Fiz Stape. The couple got together after Fiz supported Tyrone through his abusive relationship with the evil Kirsty Soames. Kirsty launched a campaign of terror on Tyrone and beat the garage mechanic black and blue. She made his life a misery with physical and mental abuse and was eventually given a prison sentence.

However, life remained far from happy for Tyrone and Fiz. In 2015 they struggled to cope when Fiz's daughter Hope was diagnosed with cancer.

Left to right: Fiz Stape [Jennie McAlpine] and Tyrone Dobbs [Alan Halsall].

MICHELLE PROPOSES TO STEVE (2015)

On the night of a charity auction in the Rovers Return, Michelle Connor passionately professed her love for Steve McDonald. In front of all the pub regulars, Michelle got down on one knee and proposed. Watched over by Sean Tully and Billy 'the vicar' Mayhew, Steve accepted Michelle's proposal. The happy couple tied the knot in 2015.

Steve's marriage to Michelle makes him *Coronation Street*'s most-wed fella, having married five women. The lucky ladies were Vicky Arden, Karen Phillips (whom he wed twice), Becky Granger, Tracy Barlow and Michelle Connor.

Left to right: Steve McDonald [Simon Gregson], Michelle Connor [Kym Marsh], Sean Tully [Antony Cotton] and Billy Mayhew [Daniel Brocklebank].

KIRK AND BETH'S
1980s WEDDING (2015)

· ·

Wedding bells rang for Kirk and Beth in 2015 when they walked down the aisle – dressed in 80s style! Beth styled herself on Madonna from her 'Like A Virgin' years. And Kirk turned up as Beth's Prince Charming, having chosen Adam Ant as his inspiration. Sally and Tim were styled as pop duo Dollar. Chesney Brown and Craig Tinker were The Blues Brothers. And Sophie Webster and Maddie Heath arrived as Vogue-style Madonna tributes, much to Beth's annoyance!

Left to right: Sophie Webster [Brooke Vincent], Maddie Heath [Amy James-Kelly], Julie Carp [Katy Cavanagh], Dev Alahan [Jimmi Harkishin], Alya Nazir [Sair Khan], Sinead Tinker [Katie McGlynn], Beth Sutherland [Lisa George], Dot Sutherland [Susie Baxter], Kirk Sutherland [Andrew Whyment], Eric Sutherland [Steve Money], Maria Connor [Samia Ghadie], Chesney Brown [Sam Aston], Craig Tinker [Colson Smith], Tracy Barlow [Kate Ford], Agnes Tinker [Juliette Kaplan], Arlene Tinker [Alison Burrows] and Nancy Tinker [Kate Fitzgerald].

WILL SALLY BE JILTED? (2015)

Weatherfield window cleaner Tim Metcalfe was horrified to discover that fiancée Sally Webster had kissed her ex, Kevin. Tim was so upset that he called off his wedding to Sally.

Sally, played by Sally Dynevor, begged Tim to turn up at their nuptials in the Bistro, but Tim refused, saying she'd be a laughing stock if she went ahead. Undeterred, Sally forged ahead with her plans, convinced that Tim would arrive. Rita Tanner tried to convince Sally that she was on a hiding to nothing with Tim and needed to admit defeat. But Sally's resolve held and she waited and waited… until Tim finally arrived.

Sally and Tim became the first *Coronation Street* couple to marry in the Bistro.

THE NAZIRS (2016)

....

The Nazirs are the most recent family to move in to Coronation Street. They live at No. 6 – along with Sharif's chickens who have taken up residence in the back garden.

After the death of gym owner Kal Nazir in the fire at Victoria Court, Kal's children Alya and Zeedan now live with their grandparents Yasmeen and Sharif. Teenager Zeedan has become smitten with Rana, a friend of his sister Alya's whom she met at university. When Rana offered to cook a meal for the Nazirs, Alya couldn't help but admire her friend's shameless schmoozing.

Left to right: Rana Habeeb [Bhavna Limbachia], Zeedan Nazir [Qasim Ahktar], Sharif Nazir [Marc Anwar] and Alya Nazir [Sair Khan].

BLACKMAIL IN THE BISTRO (2016)

Blackmail and deception are second nature to someone as evil as Tracy Barlow. When she discovered that Carla Connor had been unfaithful to fiancé Nick Tilsley by sleeping with Robert Preston, Tracy told Carla to leave Weatherfield or she'd tell Nick the truth. Carla persuaded Nick to sell the Bistro so they could move away and Robert expressed interest in buying the place. But Robert was unable to raise the funds – and that's when Carla gave Tracy cash to give to Robert so that her secret would be safe. Unfortunately for Carla, her secrets were aired on her wedding day to Nick and she left the cobbles a broken woman.

Left to right: Robert Preston [Tristan Gemmill], Tracy Barlow [Kate Ford], Nick Tilsley [Ben Price] and Carla Connor [Alison King].

ACKNOWLEDGEMENTS

Octopus Publishing Group would like to thank the Coronation Street production team; Dominic Khouri, Kieran Roberts, Helen Nugent and everyone in the Manchester office; Ashleigh Batchelar and Shirley Patton; Ellie Cullen, Danny and Nick at KJA Artists; and Faye Lehane.

PICTURE CREDITS